Whispers of the Sea

Juliana Stewart

Blessings!
Juliana Stewart

From the Balcony Publishing
Dallas, Texas

From the Balcony Publishing
25 Highland Park Village, #100-403
Dallas, TX 75205

For more information regarding special discounts for bulk purchases, please contact the publisher at 903-363-3993 or by e-mail at info@whispersoftheseabook.com

A goodmedia communications, llc book. www.goodmediacommunications.com
Cover & Book Design by goodmedia communications, llc
Author photograph by Pure 7 Studios

The text in this book is set in Book Antiqua and Edwardian Script

Printed by Taylor Publishing: Certified and audited by the Sustainable Forestry Initiative (SFI) and Programme for the Endorsement of Forest Certification (PEFC).

Manufactured in the United States of America.
Library of Congress Cataloging-in-Publication Data

    Stewart, Juliana.
      Whispers of the sea / Juliana Stewart.
      p. cm.
      LCCN 2010936119
      ISBN-13: 9780982963500
      ISBN-10: 0982963505

      1. Self-actualization (Psychology) 2. Religious
    life. 3. Women and the sea. 4. Meditations.
    I. Title.

    BF637.S4S74 2010   158.1
                QBI10-600180

For my husband David and sons Alvie and Ross

Table of Contents

Table of Contents

Acknowledgments

In honor and loving memory of my mother who taught me the Way, the Truth and the Life through Jesus.

I would like to thank my husband David; if it were not for his encouraging words "go to the beach and enjoy," I would not have written this book. I thank him for his support and never-ending patience. He is the love of my life, my soul mate, and the one who understands me enough to help me understand myself. I love you, David.

I would also like to thank my two sons, Alvie and Ross, for teaching me to love unconditionally. I love you the most.

To my artist and friend, Davilla Harding, thank you for your perception, creativity, and diligence. You are truly a blessing.

To Robyn Short of goodmedia communications, thank you for your constant smile, enduring patience and desire for excellence. You are a godsend!

I would also like to thank my spiritual ministers, Billy Cissell and Hygeia Patrick, for your love, prayers, wisdom and friendship. God bless you both.

To Debra McGee, my business partner and dear friend, you are truly a blessing from God. Thank you for spending your time taking care of business and allowing me to spend mine writing.

To Tamra Lichtenberg, a friend and a diamond, thank you for lending me your grandfather's favorite saying: "Friends are like jewels but diamonds are rare, and we only get a few in our life."

To my family, my sisters Cathy and Danna (Susie) and my brother Jay, thank you for being my forever friends; to my father for his teaching and unconditional love; to my niece and nephews for bringing joy to my life; and my brother-in-laws, thank you for putting up with our family.

I love you all.

Introduction

Those who live by the sea can hardly form a single thought of which the sea would not be part." ~Hermann Broch

Go out and stand on the mountain in the presence of the Lord, for the Lord is about to pass by.

Then a great and powerful wind tore the mountains apart and shattered the rocks before the Lord, but the Lord was not in the wind. After the wind, there was an earthquake, but the Lord was not in the earthquake. After the earthquake came a fire, but the Lord was not in the fire. And after the fire came a gentle whisper.

1 Kings 19:11-12

40 Days by the Sea

To listen for the "whispers" that speak to our soul, sometimes we must find a place our soul calls home—a place we can go to be still and listen. The place my soul calls home is on a balcony overlooking the sea.

I am not suggesting a balcony—or even an ocean—is required for hearing His voice. One might look for Him in a garden, on a mountaintop, or in a prayer closet at home, and He faithfully answers. It is when we seek quiet solitude, listen and are still, the Spirit of Truth whispers to our hearts, and we find in solitude that we are never alone.

Like a true friend, He waits on my balcony and invites me to sit and listen as He teaches about His nature.

My Balcony

From my balcony each day, I watch the Artist paint a colorful array of magical sunrises and sunsets. I feel the presence of the Creator as I look out over the vastness of the sea.

The ocean's tide inhales and exhales as if it is the very breath of God. Like a true friend, He waits on my balcony and invites me to sit and listen as He teaches about His nature.

I sit for a while, blocking out sounds and distractions, listening intently to the music of the sea. The rhythm lulls and rocks me like a child resting in her father's arms.

I hear the small still voice, a whisper that resonates across the water, speaking to my spirit and singing to my soul.

At night in bed, I often hear the whispers of the sea calling, inviting me to come to the balcony and listen.

When I look out toward the horizon, I see Him: the Creator, the Artist, the Master.

When I listen, I hear Him: the Teacher, the Father, the Friend.

15

Be Still

The waves gracefully roll onto the seashore. I hear the sounds of His whisper: gentle, steady, and never-ending.

In the distance, I hear the crow reminding me of the nemesis of my soul. He distracts with his incessant chatter. He laughs and taunts as he tries to keep me from the serenity of God. I ignore him. He taunts and laughs even louder and distracts repeatedly. I still my mind, pondering on the beauty of the sea, and ignore him until he finally flies away.

I look out once again and see the vast ocean, and once more I listen:

Be still and know that I am God, He whispers.

I lift my eyes to the heavens in admiration. The ever-changing sky is His canvas, painted in palettes of blue. His light illuminates the white clouds. As the sun rises, golden sunlight filters through the clouds, reminding me of His presence.

Be still and know that I am God, I remember … so, I am still.

I rest now with the lover of my soul. I am with the one I love, and He is with me.

He whispers, *I am here.*

I whisper back, *I know.*

We go to museums and observe art to perceive the heart of the artist. The same concept holds true of the sea when we gaze into the creation and reflect upon the Creator.

The Master

*A*mber rays of sunlight flicker across the balcony, and the brilliance of the day surrounds me in quiet serenity. Only by the hand of the Divine is such beauty created. As I silently look out over the expansive horizon, the sea beckons me to look inward. Listening to the music of God, I feel a gentle breeze blowing, refreshing my spirit. The sun glistens in the east, glowing orange across the waves as the Master displays His work of art.

In the distance, a tanned, young man with blonde hair walks his black labrador retriever. He stops to take in the tranquility, quietly watching the waves flow upon the sand. I too, watch from the balcony.

We go to museums and observe art to perceive the heart of the artist. The same concept holds true of the sea when we gaze into the creation and reflect upon the Creator. Somewhere amongst the sapphire, turquoise, and emerald waves lie the answers to our questions in the ever-changing glory of the sea.

I once heard a story of a monk who asked his students to stare at a rose for hours to observe God's creation. When the

time was up, the lesson was over. Similarly, the sea is to be studied and admired.

I reflect upon the scenery of last evening … I walked the beach as the sun set, and the water glimmered in an effervescent blue that sparkled across the entire ocean. The darkness of the sky provided a canvas for a watercolor, bleeding together yellows, oranges, smoky grays, and shades of blue. I tried to capture the colors of the sky with my lens, but when I looked at the photos, I realized no justice was done. I committed it to memory instead. I know I will always remember the vibrant colors fading into the dark night.

Again today, the sea is captivating and mesmerizing.

I will spend my day walking and contemplating the Master and His masterpiece.

21

I close my eyes, His peace surrounds me, and I remember that I am never alone.

Peace

Translucent waves gently touch the shore while the ocean seems perfectly still just a few feet away. The color turquoise against the white sand calms my spirit, and a warm, tranquil breeze brings peace to my soul.

Many people fight solitude; many consider the absence of another person to be a form of rejection or alienation. However, being alone allows us to spend time with Him ... to listen, to quiet our minds, to meditate, and to rest.

As I look out over the ocean, my soul delights within me. I am at peace.

In my view, a lone seagull reminds me of a kindred spirit. We both enjoy quiet solitude; he contemplates his world as I contemplate mine. Two men have come to gaze upon the shore. They stand still without words.

As the tide breathes in and out, the whispers of the sea entice me to listen. I gaze into the heavens and remember He is the beginning and the end, the Creator of all heaven and earth, and the Creator of my soul.

I close my eyes. His peace surrounds me, and I remember that I am never alone.

I love the constant sounds of the sea ... those sounds are imprinted in my soul, the voice that speaks to my heart and understands my spirit.

The Place My Soul Calls Home

I have returned to the sea; the place I love. I rediscover the best of myself here. I feel renewed and relaxed—in my element. I love the constant sounds of the sea ... those sounds are imprinted in my soul, the voice that speaks to my heart and understands my spirit.

In the gentle wind, the breath of God whispers hope for tomorrow.

The soft waves caress the shore, and a myriad of untraceable footprints decorate its border. Beneath a sunny sky, the ocean promises a clear and colorful presentation of blue.

I feel the white sand under my feet, and the water gently brushes against my ankles. The sun's radiance warms my soul, and my spirit soars like the seagulls above.

I look out over the ocean's waves beyond the horizon and thank God for this place ... the place my soul calls home.

Free Indeed

Today, while sitting on my balcony contemplating life, I observed a woman strolling along the beach. As alone in her world as I was in mine, she suddenly twirled in a dance-like motion, several times in joyful glee. I thought how wonderful it is to be so free. Yet, many people remain in bondage rather than choosing freedom. Through wisdom, we learn freedom is a choice.

We each have within us the freedom to choose happiness over sadness and a positive attitude no matter the circumstance.

We have the freedom to rejoice in God and trust Him even when the world seems to be falling apart.

We have the freedom to choose to love those who persecute us, knowing the height to which love will lift us as opposed to the depth of poverty that anguishes our spirits when we choose to hate.

We have the freedom to choose faith over worry, reversing the spell that overshadows our souls with darkness the moment worry steps in.

Freedom comes when we realize it is not about us ... but entirely about Him. Peace flows like a river, and His love permeates our souls … changing us and setting us free.

Now I see my friend, the dancer, singing and dancing—free indeed!

She has no idea someone else rejoices in her freedom.

If only we would show as much grace as the sand upon the shore, and forgive as quickly as the ocean's waves, then perhaps we might learn yet another lesson from the sea.

Words of the Heart

The sun shimmers across the water. All is quiet. The ocean reflects the majesty of the sky, and the tide dampens the shoreline. I notice a young boy writing his name in the sand. As the waves wash it away, he runs toward his father.

I wish unkind words could be washed away like the young boy's name in the sand. However, they often leave an indelible mark upon our hearts.

Sometimes, expectations get in our way, and we say words we later regret. Expressing our true feelings can make us vulnerable, but not sharing our feelings can leave us empty. Often we mean one thing, yet say another. I have found listening to the heart better than listening to words. The heart is more truthful.

At times, anger steps in and we cannot hear the other person because our own thoughts continue to play like an old recording we simply do not erase. It is difficult to trust the intentions of another when harsh words are spoken, but we must if the relationship is to endure. Trust is a gift, and forgiveness is always our test.

If only we would show as much grace as the sand upon the shore and forgive as quickly as the ocean's waves, then perhaps we might learn yet another lesson from the sea.

A Time for Everything

There is a time for everything ... A time to be born and a time to die.
Ecclesiastes 3:2

It appears the sun forgot to shine today; the ocean hides in the mist of the morning. The Artist chose not to paint. He washed the canvas with grays, leaving no distinction between the sky and the sea. He left the colors of the palette to yesterday's memory. The whispering of the waves against the shore and the singing birds in the nearby palms remind me that all is well, even if the world seems colorless today.

High humidity dampens the day while a warm breeze blows. The balcony is too wet; so I watch the ocean from the bedroom window as I wait for the sun.

Waiting is hard ... waiting for the sun to shine, waiting for the results from tests, waiting for your new baby to take his first breath, or waiting and wondering when your father will take his last. The clock is often not our friend, ticking like a bomb that is waiting to explode. We ignore the ticking and try to get used to it, but sometimes the sound is so loud we must hide it in a closet or under the bed so as not to listen to its incessant clatter. So often, we spend our time inconvenienced, waiting on something or someone. We would rather run ahead than wait. I do not know anyone who likes to wait—just those who seem

31

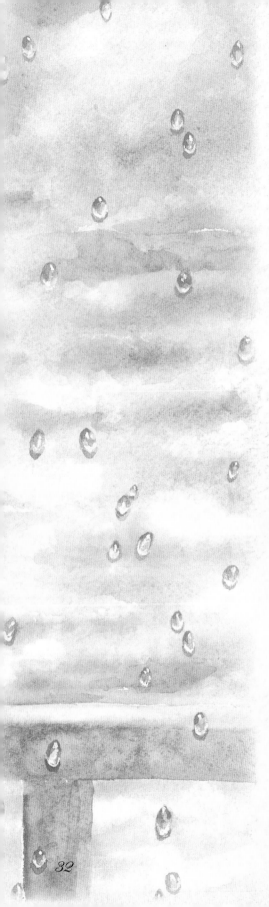

more patient than others.

Some days we would prefer to speed up the clock while other days we wish we could slow it down. As we age, we often reflect upon our lives and wish we had more time.

The Bible states, *There is a time for everything. A time to be born and a time to die.* Since our strongest instinct is self-preservation, we fight against death with all our might, and yearn to live another day.

We each have an appointment with the Lord … a day to no longer fight against time or experience the frustration of waiting. Instead, when He beckons, we will close our eyes and go home. We will not wait, even if the timing seems utterly inconvenient.

He must have loved her more than life, but now life goes on without her. All he has are memories.

The Stranger

A smoky fog paints the heavens and earth with a silver mist. I hear the sounds of the waves crashing upon the seashore, yet the ocean appears to have vanished into the night.

Standing on my balcony, I notice the humidity has saturated the wicker furniture, and dampness hangs in the air. I can barely make out the whitecaps as they play against the shoreline. Later the fog will lift, and the sun will shine—just as on all days, hope is attainable.

Although it takes longer, it seems like mere moments before broken sunlight filters through the darkness, and the teal blue ocean appears. The fog lifts almost instantly. Then, I see him from a distance ... a stranger unaware.

He appears to have come seeking answers. His grief seems great as I watch him weep ... his tears become one with the ocean.

He may be thinking of regrets or solitude. His love and loss are evident. He must have loved her more than life, but now life goes on without her. All he has are memories.

He appears to ponder the questions that have no answers; even the whispers of the sea cannot be heard above his sobs.

I imagine they walked many times on these shores, hand-in-hand. Surely he knows life is short, but life without her must now seem so long.

My tears begin to flow as I pray in silence and watch him slowly walk away. Today, two strangers met without saying a word.

The Pursuit

The tide glides onto the shore, and the brilliant sun reflects upon a crystal blue sea. A seagull takes flight over the water as the sea glistens beneath his wings. I hear the echo of his laughter and the soothing sounds of the waves. Sometimes I think I could stay here forever.

The gentleness of the ocean reminds me of all that is kind and good, like the soothing whispers of a mother to her child. I feel as if I have been in a cocoon or wrapped in swaddling clothes while I have been here—sheltered, relaxed, reborn.

The Lord is so close, I sense His presence. It is as if can I hear His heart beating, coming closer, and encircling me. I cannot move. I feel hemmed in. I cannot breathe. I hear His gentle whispers speaking a love language ... calling to my soul. I hear distractions. The crow chatters, perched on the flagpole. The neighbors talk boisterously. From people I have never noticed before, I hear noise. The crow continues his taunting chatter. The seagull's laugh is now in a high pitch.

I drown out the sounds and wait. I think about regrets and about how I would have done things differently. I ask for forgiveness. Yet, that is not His quest.

He is pursuing me, closing in. I have felt this before when struggling to make a decision. Today, there is no struggle—just His heartbeat and His whisper. Weak and unable to stand, I feel my own heart beat rapidly in my chest and I pray: *Change my heart so that I might pursue You as You have pursued me.*

Storms

The heavens are angry, and the ocean rages. Strong winds prevent me from opening the door and enjoying the day on the balcony. I stare out the window as beads of rain blur the view. Watching white waves crash against the shore and listening to the gusty winds howl outside, I long for a sunny, beautiful day. Instead, torrential rains come down, and the ocean churns.

I reflect upon turbulent days in my life—the days I would have rather stayed inside and not confronted the problems at hand. Most days, we must go out into the weather to face life head-on when we would rather crawl back into bed. However, today I can sit and watch from the safety of my window.

There are so many pressures in life: finances, work, health, children, parents, and lovers. As the scripture states: *The rain falls on the just and the unjust alike.* It is relative; problems are problems with no measuring device that tells us which ones are worse. Pain is pain in any form. Disappointments come and go. *That's life*, they say.

In a perfect world, we would have sunshine, a blue sky, and a turquoise sea every day. However, without the storms, how would we appreciate the difference?

Sometimes we bring on our own storms, creating such problems that consequences are inevitable. I have learned there will always be both storms and consequences. How we endure them, and deal with the aftermath, is the true test.

When tears fall like the rain, we must dry our eyes, take out our umbrellas, and face the weather with the strength and grace of a woman ... strong enough to survive any storm.

Forgiveness

The moon suspends in the heavens while lavender fades behind the horizon. The blue sky becomes bluer as the melody of the ocean calms my spirit. Every sunrise brings forth the rebirth of hope and expectation. It is a new day—a day to put yesterday behind us. Today has just been born like a new baby coming into the world from his mother's womb.

Each day, He allows us to start over—to try again. The rising sun casts colors of rose, pink, and brilliant orange as it shines through the morning sky, marking the beginning of life in this new day. With each new day, we must make time to forgive the mistakes of yesterday, remembering we only have one day at a time, one moment at a time, to do the best we can.

I think how one person's best may be different from another's. Our lot in life, our fate, is somehow created from a tapestry we have woven. The culmination of life carries us to this place in time, this now, this new beginning. We will never journey upon the same path again. Each moment is like a grain of sand on the beach—unique. We would change some moments, if we could; others we will cherish forever. I find it best to hold on to the good and to let go of the bad. Life seems easier this way, and it wears less on our faces and on our hearts.

47

We all seem to have days that change our lives forever. Each life has a different story, but no one escapes the cruelties of those days that forever change us. To look back and think *if only* is self-punishment that leads to torture. So, with each new day comes a new beginning—a chance to forgive ourselves, as well as others.

Forgiveness fills my heart as the sun climbs, lavender fades, and the sea turns a deeper shade of blue.

Today, I will walk down to the shore, stand beside the seagull, face the wind, and place my footprints in the sand.

Facing the Wind

The brisk wind blows from the west, and the turbulent white waves thunder against the shore. I remain protected on my balcony, wrapped in a warm blanket. I hear the crow; his call reminds me of his presence. The seagulls stand on the beach and enjoy the sun. They face the wind, contemplating flight. One spreads his wings and hovers over the water in anticipation of breakfast.

The footprints on the sand have been washed away, leaving no traces of yesterday. The only prints that remain on this cool morning are those of the seagulls—not a person nor a dog, just the seagulls.

In quiet contemplation, I try to clear my mind and allow the coolness of the air to awaken me. Still groggy, no thoughts come as in days before. I missed the morning sun, and last evening's sunset escaped me. My thoughts move inward, focused on the pains of my body, as my mind submits. I have only this day. Though my body hurts, my mind is unclear, and I would rather crawl back into bed, I will not ... for I might miss the best day of my life.

Today, I will walk down to the shore, stand beside the seagull, face the wind, and place my footprints in the sand.

I notice how the horizon appears to end, allowing us to see only so far ... a wonderful illustration of how we should live one day at a time.

Patience

Reminiscent of an Impressionist painting, only one wave approaches the shore. No one strolls along the beach; either it is too early or too cool. I watch the sun glistening in the east, filtering through the palm trees casting shadows on the balcony. I gaze out onto the hazy horizon and listen for the gentle whisper of the sea. Patiently I wait, hoping to hear His voice. All is quiet.

I notice how the horizon appears to end, allowing us to see only so far—a wonderful illustration of how we should live one day at a time. Sometimes, we look toward the future—anxiously—living for tomorrow while not paying attention to today. It is easy to race toward our goals and lose sight of the present. We prefer to do something, anything. Taking action feels better than being still. The Bible teaches, *Seek, and you shall find,* yet there are times when we should be patient, and *Wait upon the Lord.*

It takes patience to be still, to breathe, and listen for the gentle whispers. We have plenty of time to do, and less time to listen. Even when there are no whispers, we find lessons in the sea.

I look out onto the shimmering ocean, and in silence, I study. Today, it seems the Teacher chose to paint instead of speak.

Prayer

The heavens command the stage with periwinkle blue illuminating the gentle clouds as they dance across the sky. The heavy rains have moved to the west, and the sea remains unsettled, waiting on the sky to dictate this day. The wind rests as if in quiet meditation. The cool breeze of yesterday is gone, and the warmth of sunshine on my face encourages me to be still like the wind.

Quietly, the seagulls fly above. The crow appears, perching on the flagpole for a moment before he flies away. Far away, I see a gray-haired man walking his snow white dog. Workers line up blue and white beach chairs in anticipation of a sunny day, though the weatherman said the rains would return.

Life, like the weather, is not so predictable. Even when we see a storm on the horizon, God may intervene. Mysteriously, the Creator of the universe allows us to change our lives through His gift of prayer.

A person who intercedes knows through obedience and timing that when heaven meets earth—as quickly as lightning flashes across the sky—a miracle may occur. This does not happen often, as we seldom get the timing right. However,

when we do, prayer can change a seemingly impossible situation.

The combination of faith, obedience, and timing speaks to the heart of God.

He hears us, and at the most unpredictable moment, He moves heaven and earth to answer our prayers.

Our children birth love into us as we birth life into them, and the umbilical cord of love is never severed.

Unconditional Love

The bright sun shimmers upon the peaceful tide. A mother and child stroll hand-in-hand taking in the tranquility of the sea. The tide brings the gentle blue waves closer today. Its movement mesmerizes, like the rocking of a cradle.

I sit on the balcony, absorbing the beauty around me as I think about a mother's love. Mothers know us best, loving us in spite of our faults.

We seldom find unconditional love upon this earth, yet love cannot express itself more fully than when a child comes into our lives. Loving a child changes us, bringing forth emotions we never knew existed. Children are our treasures. We carry them in our wombs and in our souls. They birth love into us as we birth life into them, and the umbilical cord of love is never severed.

My attention turns back to the mother and child still strolling hand-in-hand. Although, I cannot make out their faces from the balcony, I see their love shining forth as brightly as the sun, and it warms my heart. Their radiant joy reflects upon my face. I smile, remembering those I love unconditionally.

The sun shines,
the sea whispers, and
I hear the seagulls
laugh ...

White Linen

I walk the sandy beach and feel the warmth of the vibrant sun upon my bare shoulders. The breeze blows my hair as the cool air awakens me from my dreams. I feel refreshed, cleansed, crisp, and renewed like the white linen that clothes my body.

What more could I want than the sea in all its glory?

White waves gently bathe the shore as rays of sunlight cast silvery shadows upon the sand. In the distance, a lone man stands at the walkway and gazes out at the sea. He turns his head as though he would rather not face the reality of his world. He stands in silence for a long time, and then slowly walks away.

We come to the sea to find the answers. It soothes our pain, replenishes our souls, and restores our spirits. The questions are our companions and the seagulls our teachers.

I wear garments of white linen, walking the shores and listening to the whispers of the sea. When I return to reality, I will take out my white linen from time to time, close my eyes, and remember. Eventually, the routine of my daily wear will take its place, and the white linen will be put on the shelf ... for another day.

When I think of my life, I feel like a lover torn between two worlds—one is serenity, the other reality.

However, today the sun shines, the sea whispers, and I hear the seagulls laugh and call my name. I face the water, close my eyes and breathe in the instantly recognizable smells of the sea. Slowly, I open my eyes and see the white linen clinging to my body. I realize that today I have chosen serenity as my reality.

63

Adversity

I walk this morning with my face to the wind. I think of adversity, how sometimes it hits us in the face as we walk against the wind. Then, with some awakening, we change course and walk with the wind at our backs and the sun on our shoulders. Sometimes we do not think to change course, although we often have no choice.

As I walk the white shore, I observe something that does not belong in the sea. Approaching, I see a dead tree laying on the edge where the water meets the sand. It seems out of place. I stop to watch my friend the seagull when I notice a small woman coming towards me with an obvious handicap. I can see her body is gnarled and twisted. With great determination and a bright smile, she speaks, "Good morning."

I think how she must have embraced adversity, and now she calls it friend. I smile back, and reply, "Good morning." Looking out to the sea, I realize that adversity comes in many forms—each of us has a different story.

This stranger on the sand causes me to pause, count my blessings, and appreciate that my circumstances can change with the wind. Her genuine smile reminds me to be thankful. She challenges me to see adversity from a different perspective.

I look down toward the tree; it too reminds me that we all seem a little out of place. With that thought in mind, I change my course, turn my face toward the sun, and follow my footprints back to the balcony.

Finding Ourselves

It is the start of a new workweek for most. Not a soul is on the beach, just traces of footprints from yesterday. The ebbing tide touches the shore, leaving a faint watermark on the sand. The delicately painted heavens display hints of blue sky with patches of white clouds.

Looking out onto the horizon, I watch the sun make its appearance, and I notice movement in the water. All at once, dolphins appear, gliding up and down, playing and entertaining. Mesmerized, I lean toward the railing on my balcony hoping to get a better look. Joy is in the air. The seagulls land, and one laughs aloud, reminding all of this new day and filling it with laughter.

It is a fairy tale of sorts to be entertained by the great sea on a day-to-day basis, although I observe some of the locals have lost the sense of wonder and are ready to return inland. I see the enchantment in the eyes of others who know why they came.

The sea helps us find our true selves, the unique individual we all wish to be: lighthearted, carefree, and fun-loving. Yet, some people—who I will never understand—say they do not care for life at the beach. I wonder if they have sat in quiet

contemplation and watched a sunset across the sea magically display its splendor or stopped long enough to watch a child build a sand castle just to have a wave wash it away and then smile anyway. Perhaps they did not pay attention to the lovers strolling hand-in-hand with a new beginning, or maybe they missed the elderly person walking the shore determined to live another day?

Joy fills each moment, creating enough memories for all to share.

If we learn to play as the dolphins, laugh like the seagulls, and smile with the children, we will surely find ourselves along the way.

Deep within two souls, the treasure of friendship shines forth to brighten our days, and illuminate even our darkest nights.

Friendship

This evening as I walk barefoot in the sand, the full moon illuminates the sky and glistens like a diamond across the water. From horizon to shore, it appears as though God has painted the sea with only one brush stroke. The light slowly fades by the hand of God, while the sun magically dances with the moon upon a crystal sea. Through the whitewashed clouds, their union brings forth the colors of precious jewels: emeralds, sapphires, and diamonds.

I watch their final performance before the sun bows and the moon takes the stage. As the curtain falls and the colors of the day vanish, only the image of diamonds remains in the night, sparkling across the sea. The majestic sky surrounds me as I think of friendships—those precious jewels given as gifts from God.

Our truest friends, our diamonds, love us in spite of ourselves. They defend our causes no matter what they may be, and they keep even our deepest secrets. Our kindred spirits bring laughter into our lives and fill our hearts with love.

Deep within two souls, the treasure of friendship shines forth to brighten our days and illuminate even our darkest nights.

Melancholy

The ocean resembles a black and white photograph—void of color, a blank canvas, empty—waiting for the Artist to take His brush and paint a new day. The sun does not shine, and the clouds are low.

I catch the crow out of the corner of my eye. He steals my attention for the moment.

A young boy and his mother cautiously approach the shore. The boy has his orange pail in tow. They stop, perhaps realizing today may not be a day to build castles in the sand. The wind roars as the two retrace their steps from the water's edge. I too believe I have had enough, and so I retreat from the beach to the haven that leads to my balcony.

It is a day to ponder life, to be introspective I suppose, knowing not every day will be sunny and bright. There are days when gray skies cast shadows that drain all the color from the sea, and today is just one of those days.

Is there another who loves to watch the sun majestically fall into the sea … who loves to gaze at the twinkling stars while looking for the Man in the Moon?

Am I Alone?

Is there anyone who loves the sounds of the ocean more than I do?

Is there anyone who appreciates the colors of the sea or the sun bursting through the sky more?

Have you created someone else that loves the sun brushing against his cheek while the tide bathes his feet?

Is there another who loves to watch the sun majestically fall into the sea … who loves to gaze at the twinkling stars while looking for the Man in the Moon?

Is there another as mesmerized by his footprints in the sand?

Can you find another who loves to watch the children build sand castles and the elderly couple stroll hand-in-hand?

Is there another who loves to paint with words while listening to the whispers of the sea?

Have you created another?

Am I alone?

The pressures of my life seem hidden ... much like a new image painted over a worn and weary canvas with the semblance of the old picture beneath.

The Mask

Gracefully painted white clouds dance across a baby blue sky, and the sea appears bluer than in previous days. The moon hides behind the clouds as it ascends into the sky. Flocks of seagulls face the ocean, and a cool breeze blows across the balcony. Not a soul walks the beach. The ocean makes its own music while the wind sings in harmony.

A seagull glides toward my balcony, alone in the sky. The rest of the flock waits on the ground. A brave one, I think, to get out of his comfort zone and take flight. The creative side of me yearns to fly with him, to be above this world, spreading my wings. Some days, I would rather fly to another shore, yet other days I think it is better to stay.

The pressures of my life seem hidden ... much like a new image painted over a worn and weary canvas with the semblance of the old picture beneath. The evidence of that life is etched on my face; a smile often covers pain, acting as a mask, presented to those I do not trust. How often we pretend.

On my balcony, there is no pretense, no mask, and no one to impress.

Perfect Love

The vivid sunlight glistens upon the shimmering water. The seagulls laugh as they glide above the shore. A gentle voice whispers, speaking a language that calls to my soul.

A young couple walks along the beach. They stop. He places his arms around her as they admire the beauty of the sea together. From the balcony, it appears they are in love.

I think about love … the give and take required. True love means placing another before ourselves and loving them unselfishly. Often, we fail to find this kind of love. Because of previous pain inflicted by another, we choose not to give ourselves completely. Instead, we continue to bandage wounds that should have healed long ago.

A friend once said, "Love means giving another person what he or she needs." I believe this can work if reciprocated, but often one takes care of the other's needs simply to become lost in the process. The balance comes when each has what they need … sometimes it is freedom.

Although perfect love seems unattainable this side of heaven, we try to love completely. It takes courage to become vulnerable enough to fall in love, but as the Bible teaches, *There is no fear in love. But perfect love drives out fear.*

My attention turns back to the fearless couple. He sweetly kisses her cheek as they walk out of sight. I take a deep breath and sigh … it seems love lingers in the air.

Marriage

I t rained last night, and turbulence fills the water. The waves restlessly beat the sand and return to sea. I rise early to observe the night transition to day. I watch as the haze disappears from the horizon and the sky turns blue. In the distance, alone on the beach, I see a couple coming closer to the balcony. As I sip my hot coffee, I wrap myself in a soft blanket, and look out again.

This time I notice the couple seems to be moving in slow motion, each at a different pace. With every step, they create more distance between themselves. It appears to be deliberate. She moves slowly behind him with her head down. She seems weary and sad, and he, oblivious or emotionally detached.

I wonder about their life together. Have they lost their way? Have they lost their joy like a seashell buried deep within the sand? Have they come to the coast one last time hoping to find it, to reclaim their love? I close my eyes, allowing the cool air to brush against my face, and think how easily we become disillusioned.

When I open my eyes and look up, I see two pelicans flying above the balcony. They remind me of marriage—the union of two hearts, flying as one over the same shore.

The strength of marriage has to be God. How else can it be? Two hearts uniting as one ... the concept is hard for most to grasp. Yet, the molding of the two in matrimony is a concept we accept.

There are cloudy days in marriage. Sometimes the rains fall and the winds blow, causing more damage than two hearts can ever mend. There are too many floods and too much water passes under the bridge. Marriage is the joining of two hearts, but often just one tries to hold the marriage together. The other would rather find another shore and bluer water—a place that is clear, unblemished, and free of debris or clutter. After all, the gray waters come from the turbulence within. Along the other shore, no turbulence occurs, and so the water remains blue.

For a second time, I notice the pelicans flying above; this time they appear closer than before. Perhaps the couple will look toward heaven, learn from the pelicans, and fly in unison once more.

The Call of the Sea

Rays of golden sunlight pour through the window and awaken me from my dreams. The hushed sound of the sea is enticing as I walk onto the balcony and feel the warm sun upon my face. I have missed this warmth, the way the sun tingles and penetrates to the depth of my soul.

The colors of the sea are exquisite this morning—shades of emeralds, jades, and sapphires.

The sea soothes as if calling my name.

Last night I heard the call. I came out onto the balcony, and in the darkness, I heard the music of the ocean. I shut my eyes and remembered the colors of the day, the way God painted the blazing sunset in shades of orange and crimson. I watched the sun disappear in a burst of magic into the sea. I saw the stars shimmering in the sky and wondered why sometimes I forget to look up and admire them. As I gazed into the starlit heavens with gratitude in my heart, I felt His glory surround me.

Again today, I feel grateful. High above, I hear the seagulls laughing, singing in harmony with the ocean's chorus. There is no laughter like that of the seagulls. The cares of this life seem to fly away on their wings.

Once again, in the rhythm of the sea, I hear His voice singing to my soul. I close my eyes and breathe in as I savor the serenity around me. Perhaps today is the most beautiful day of all.

I see the footprints of those who wander around, going nowhere, and I ask: Am I on the same path?

Footprints That Lead Nowhere

It is cold, but the wind is still and the sun shines. I long for glimpses of blue in the ocean, yet it appears colorless today. Ripples of white break up waves of gray, and a few seagulls gather on a hushed shore.

I question why I am here.

Perhaps I need to listen.

Am I on course?

Have I gone astray?

What lessons should I learn?

I see the footprints of those who wander around, going nowhere, and I ask:

Am I on the same path?

Is my life like those footprints that lead nowhere?

Miracles

I awoke early, pulled back the drapes, and watched the colors of the morning sun paint the eastern sky with shades of rose and hues of yellow. Bundled up in a blanket, I watched the sun rise from the balcony while the full moon, still high in the heavens, made no apologies for not relinquishing the sky.

Now, the crystal blue of the sea entreats me as I watch the seagulls fly in and circle gracefully. I intend to watch the sun rise and set as many days as possible.

Last evening, I walked the beach in my sandals, my feet cold in the night air. I stood in silence watching the lavender sunset. I prayed as I watched the sun descend into the majestic sea. I thought about how I very seldom take time to watch this incredible act of God. When I do, I often forget to pay homage to the most High God.

I consider the faith of the natives who knew no better than to worship the sun, who believed there was a God, and who believed in the splendor of the sun and in the light of the moon. Thus, they worshipped the created while looking for the Creator. God must yearn for us to continue our search for Him.

The miracles of God seem so close, yet we forget to watch

the flower bloom or the mother bird feeding her baby. We forget to look at the stars and imagine the vastness of the universe ... the galaxies unexplored. We each live in our own little world. We believe we are the masters of our fate and continue as if no one else exists. We tend to think our problems are the most significant—perhaps they are. Yet God, in His infinite wisdom, continues to be faithful. He shines His glory on all who seek Him.

I look out onto the crystal sea, as the sun glistens across the iridescent water, and it appears as though He shines His glory down from heaven ... just for me.

Contentment

Come, He whispers. I meet Him once again on my balcony. He is faithful, and thus far, so am I. The warmth of heaven shines upon my face.

Sunlight flickers across the water, illuminating the colors of the sea ... soft turquoise in the midst of white waves—the colors of contentment. Strokes of ivory clouds are painted across the soft blue sky, and amber rays of sunshine reflect upon the water.

Peace and tranquility blow in the breeze, and contentment fills the air.

I look out at the sea and sky dotted with specks of white seagulls, as many as the eye can see. They are content to fly against the wind, going nowhere.

I am content to stay on my balcony and listen. No one comes and goes; no one makes demands.

Almost unnoticed, the treasure of contentment radiates from the depth of my soul, reflecting upon the water like a mirror shining from above.

I feel His contentment all around me.

*As I look up,
I see their wings
above me, white and
strong, as if angels
were rushing in,
surrounding and
protecting me.*

Angels Rush In

The clouds appear a little lower than normal. The climbing sun promises blue skies and a high tide brings the shoreline closer. I see a few children walking and looking for seashells. The storm has passed, but the ocean remains restless.

The noisy crow perches on the railing of the balcony. I shun him once again, ignoring his mocking. He calls for his friends, but none come. If I ignore him, he will go away. He has little power without submission, and I have learned he must have an audience. Then once again, he leaves to annoy another.

I turn my attention to the seagulls.

As I look up, I see their wings above me, white and strong, as if angels are rushing in, surrounding and protecting me.

So often, we pray and pray, wondering why God has not heard our prayer or why He seems to be absent when we so need His presence.

Faith

An early morning fog meets the ocean's haze, appearing as an image in an out of focus lens. The muted yellow sun makes a slight appearance as the lavender fog fades. A horizon with no definition seems to disappear into the sea as a faint blue line defines the shore. The white sand looks like freshly fallen snow as the waves roll upon it. In the mist far away, an elderly man slowly walks along the beach.

Later the sun will come out in all its brilliance, and the heavy fog will burn away.

Sometimes life seems out of focus, and our thinking becomes foggy. We make bad decisions that unravel the tapestry of our lives.

I think about the pressures I have known and how I have learned to wait—knowing the right answer will come if I give it time. Sometimes the waiting is just too hard. However, when the fog lifts, we realize the answer had been there all along—we just could not see it. A compass would help determine which direction to take when the light of day has escaped. However, no compass gets us through the fog—only time and prayer.

So often, we pray and pray, wondering why God has not heard our prayer or why He seems to be absent when we so need His presence.

Life seems clearer on the balcony, even in the fog. Faith tells us even in the hardest times, the times when the fog enters our life, He is there.

We simply cannot see Him.

Ownership

Activity surrounds the balcony this morning. The white sand is adorned with people, all trying to find a perfect spot to put down their stakes for the day.

A man and a woman walk hastily by. They look like they have been married for years. The wife walks in front of her husband. He wears red slippers and a cap as if to claim, "I am still young at heart."

A little girl in a pink swimsuit works on her sand castle while her mother sits under a blue and white umbrella, engaged in her book.

The seagulls fly around, almost in a circle, spreading their wings. They call out before finally landing upon the sand.

A surfer walks cautiously to the ocean and waits for another to join him. People now stroll from the right and the left, talking, contemplating, and sharing.

I thank God that we share the coast and that all God's creation can walk without trespassing. Territorial humans stake claims and draw deeds to prove their ownership. It seems presumptuous to believe that we can own whatever our money will buy.

I question aloud, "Who owns the ocean, if not God himself?"

"Who owns the sky? Is it not God?"

Perhaps God and all the other creatures of the earth smile together, understanding the fallacy of ownership. I wonder if the seagulls know more than we do, as I watch them spread their wings and fly away to another shore.

Worship

The sun rises and seems to hover just above the palm branches. According to man, it is the Sabbath ... the day God rested. From the balcony, all is well. To the left, two men come to the beach to worship. They set up their sound equipment and begin singing praise songs. A few moments later, men and women appear with lawn chairs. I recognize some of the songs, although with the sound of the waves in the background, I find it difficult to hear all the words. Sitting in my robe on the balcony with a warm cup of coffee, I go unnoticed while they have church on the beach.

I wonder if some have come to worship, while others have come out of obligation. Who dragged their spouses along with them, and who came because of the scenery? My attention is drawn back to a woman walking on the beach in her swimsuit. She stops in reverence as the preacher begins to pray.

From the balcony, it is easy to judge the hearts of men, and surely, if they noticed me, it would be equally easy for them to judge my heart. Our human nature taints the purity of the Divine. Is it possible to worship without saying a word, to come in silent adoration of the Creator and His creation? It is often easier to talk over God than to listen for His voice ... even on Sunday morning.

Today, fear of tomorrow has no place on this shore. Instead of worry, I will remember the One who holds my future and trust Him with all the faith I have.

Fear of Tomorrow

An eerie stillness drapes the air. The crow perches himself on the flagpole, yet even he is still. The tide eases out as it leaves a water stain upon the sand. A light gray sea and a hazy horizon promise a quiet day. No one comes or goes. A few seagulls are scattered, yet they too, do not move.

Suspicious of the quiet, an unsettled feeling surfaces like the calm before a storm or a ship drifting from the harbor.

I think of the work I have left behind, in order to escape, but when I think about returning ... my spirit winces. The work is in my soul, but the love has left—as at the end of a love affair when two people continue to hold onto the memories but do not have the energy to make more.

The fear of change and the uncertainty of tomorrow cause us to hold on longer than we should. Fear robs us of our faith. Together with worry and anxiety, fear attacks when we least expect it.

Today, fear of tomorrow has no place on this shore. Instead of worry, I will remember the One who holds my future and trust Him with all the faith I have.

Like a breath of fresh air, a breeze blows across the water.

I look at the flagpole just in time to see the crow spread his wings and fly away.

Heavy Water

A mystical fog covers the balcony, only allowing glimpses of the sea to shine through. The obscured sun climbs in the sky. There are bursts of blue skies and white clouds above as the ocean sings a lullaby. The violet fog promises to lift and allow the blue sky to change the course of this day, yet heaviness fills the air. The still wind lurks, and frustrations set in.

Sometimes, we feel a heaviness as if we are drowning ... knowing only God can save us from ourselves. We realize self-reliance is unattainable when one is drowning.

Then He whispers, *The water will not overtake you.*

The wind dries our tears. We vow to change and choose not to allow the heavy thoughts or the dimly lighted day to steal our joy.

We search for peace. In time, the presence of God appears as the sun breaks through and disperses the clouds. The warmth penetrates to the depth of our souls, and we realize the sun never left the sky, nor did He leave our sides.

During those times, when the heaviness of our tears blinds our vision, we must look for Him to still the wind, dry the tears, and rescue us from drowning.

When a new day approaches, we look for the sun to shine and bring the glory of God to dissipate the dark night.

Hope

A strong wind gusts across the thunderous waters and heavy clouds blanket the sky. Hints of sunlight paint the ocean in shades of blue and violet. Some days, the clouds veil the glory of God so we cannot see. We are like children in the desert who cannot find their way. God seems to hide from us, and we wake up feeling alone. The faith we stood on yesterday disappears into the fog, and we cannot seem to find solid ground.

Sometimes we feel as though the cloudy sky will stay. We forget that the sun hides behind the clouds but will shine again. The dark clouds blind our focus, leaving us weary. The nemesis of our souls tempt us to look at the obstacle, and believe it is there to stay. When we agree with him, the obstacle tries to overtake us. It may take a long time for us to notice when the fog lifts.

The key is not to agree with the nemesis, but to lift our eyes to the One who can bring about a new day. When a new day approaches, we look for the sun to shine and bring the glory of God to dissipate the dark night. With the first glimmer of light, hope is reborn, the clouds blow away, and the sun shines upon our faces once again.

He is our redeemer ... the one who restores our hopes and delivers us out of darkness.

Consequences

The stars shine like tiny diamonds in the night, illuminating the sapphire sky. A full moon glistens upon the waves and creates the impression of a perfect evening. The removal of the sign warning of a treacherous undertow leaves little remembrance of last evening's storms.

Sometimes in life we do not heed the signs, and we ignore the inner whispers telling us to stop. The strong undertow of temptation weakens our flesh. Wisdom speaks, but we ignore it. A beautiful illusion is masked by deception, so the illusion turns to delusion.

We tend to justify the desires of our hearts instead of recognizing the heart deceives. So selfishly, we call evil good and long for more. Owning the lie is easier than turning to truth and disciplining the mind. All our choices have consequences.

What we put into life, we usually get out in ways we seldom understand.

I have learned ...
He is enough. I
need nothing more.

What More Could I Ask?

I spend my days welcoming the sun and my nights gazing into the heavens.

I watch the moon find its way on a bright day and then penetrate the dark night.

As I listen to the music of the ocean, I witness spectacular sunrises and glorious sunsets.

I walk the sandy beach, barefoot, and feel the wet sand between my toes, as the waves brush against my ankles.

I feel the warmth of the sun as I pick up seashells and place them in my pockets.

I smell the sea as it salts the air, and I savor the taste upon my lips.

I have listened to the whispers of the sea ... and fallen in love.

What more could I ask?

I have learned ... He is enough. I need nothing more.

My footprints—
ever present on
the sand—will
be washed away
by tomorrow's
tide, untraceable,
vanished, as if they
were only a dream.

A Dream

I awaken from a sound sleep before daybreak and wrestle with the morning for a few hours before falling back to sleep. I dream of the colors in the sea.

The dampness of the morning rain covers the balcony. The sun hides behind the painted clouds. A crystal blue ocean calls out to come and play, yet the mist has kept those who would normally stroll indoors. A cool breeze blows across the white, sandy shore.

When I return home, my days here will fade into one memory. My footprints, ever present on the sand, will be swept away by tomorrow's tide—untraceable, vanished, as if only a dream.

Looking out on the ocean and listening intently for the whispers that speak to my soul, I want so desperately to stay and walk these shores.

In just a few mornings, my husband will nudge me and whisper sweetly, "Time to wake up." I will wonder if this place was simply a dream, a faraway place only my subconscious remembers. I will wake to the sounds and smells of home, and I will be happy I am with the ones I love.

But ... the dream will linger.

Closing my eyes, I will see the colors and hear the sounds of the ocean. I will remember the way the sand felt under my feet and the way the gentle waves bathed my skin. I will breathe in and recall the scent of cocoa butter in the air. I will close my eyes even tighter and hear the seagulls laugh around me. I will remember the way God whispered into my ear as the breeze sent chills over my body.

I will remember, and I will wonder if this place was merely a dream.

I will have to return to it—it will not return to me. With that thought, I release the white sand from my hand and set it free.

Returning

I scoop up the white sand and let it slip through my fingers.

After a while, I scoop up enough to take home with me.

I decide I will place it in a vase to remind me of the white sands against the turquoise sea.

I will remember the way it felt beneath my feet, and I will think of it often.

If only I could capture the elusive sea, I would bottle it too, and take it with me. Soon enough though, it would evaporate— like the dream.

If I could take the footprints on the shore, or place the breeze in a bottle to release the smells of the sea when I return home, or if I could capture a seagull and take it home with me, would I?

I think not.

Instead, I will awake in my bed and see the white sand sitting in the vase thrust into my world, a little out of place.

I will recall the rest and fall back to sleep to dream a little more.

I will have to return to it—it will not return to me.

With that thought, I release the white sand from my hand and set it free.

Author's Note

The Place My Heart Calls Home

Before I left the beach, I went to my balcony overlooking the sea. As it drowned out the noise in my head, I could hear a gentle whisper. I felt His breath as soft as the breeze, His heartbeat loud and steady within me. From the balcony, I heard the whispers of the sea and when I listened intently, I heard His voice.

I have always had a love affair with the sea and often refer to it as the place my soul calls home ... but this time it was more. This time it was about Him, the lover of my soul. When it was time to leave, I felt torn between two worlds, the balcony where I met Him each day, and the reality of the long road home that would take me back to the routine of everyday life. In the twilight of the morning, I said goodbye to the sea, knowing I would have to return to it—it would not return to me.

Driving home, the time passed quickly. I knew why I not only had to leave, but wanted to leave, my true love—the one who understands me enough to allow me to understand myself, my soul mate—awaited my return.

After a long journey with only a few breaks, I drove up the winding road leading to the place my *heart* calls home. The familiar sounds of laughter and dogs barking, the smells of dinner on the stove, and my family waiting with open arms, made me question why I left. I had been away a long time, in search of my better self. Both the joys and pressures of life exist between these walls. I opened the door and walked through, realizing that while I already missed the serenity of the sea, I was ready to be home. I was ready to share reality with my family.

$\sim \sim \sim$

*B*etween the daily challenges and the occasional misunderstandings of life is unconditional love and genuine caring. Tears of joy, tears of pain, and a love that does not fail, all abide in this place my *heart* calls home.

Before long, I rediscover the balcony overlooking the gardens of our home and begin to listen. The whispers in the gardens replace the whispers of the sea, yet the voice is the same. Within days, I am writing ... on a balcony overlooking a garden in the place my *heart* calls home.

About the Author

Juliana Stewart

*J*uliana Stewart is a wife, a mother, and lover of her Creator and His creation. The next book in the *Whispers* series, *Whispers in the Gardens*, will be released soon. In the meantime, Juliana will be traveling, seeking inspiration from balconies and listening for gentle whispers. She is currently writing her first novel. *Whispers of the Sea* is her first book.